1. Introduction

Lenders of last resort today face a common moral-hazard problem: offering systemic protection without encouraging bad behavior by those who enjoy protection. Prudential regulation accompanies bank safety nets for precisely that reason. But what if some market players — typically referred to as "shadow banks" — avoid regulation while still enjoying the benefits of protection?

This is not a new problem. The Federal Reserve System was founded in 1913 to stabilize the American banking system by offering banks access to its discount window. When the Federal Reserve System was created, the Federal Reserve imposed reserve requirements and other regulations on members to ensure that banks would not take advantage of systemic protection to take undue risks. But the Federal Reserve found that many banks chose not to join its system, precisely to avoid its regulatory requirements. Indeed, less than 8 percent of all state-chartered banks (which had the option to remain outside the Federal Reserve System) chose to join the Federal Reserve during its first decade of operation.[1] Many observers, including Federal Reserve officials, politicians, and scholars, speculated that nonmember state-chartered banks were able to enjoy the benefits of Federal Reserve liquidity provision through indirect pass-throughs of discount window lending within the interbank network. In that sense, the Federal Reserve membership problem of the early 20th century is considered an early example of the moral hazard problem of shadow banking. However, before this study, there has been no quantitative analysis of the decisions by state-chartered banks to join or not join the Federal Reserve, or of the ability of nonmember banks to gain indirect access to the discount window through interbank lending.

---

[1] According to the *All Banks Statistics United States 1896-1955* (1959), there were 20,323 commercial banks in 1924, yet only 1,604 were members of the Federal Reserve as of the *Annual Report of the Federal Reserve Board* (1925) .

The creation of the Federal Reserve was intended to resolve the instability of the American banking system. The pre-Federal Reserve era was characterized by high volatility of loan interest rates at seasonal frequency and frequent episodes of banking panics. [2] Before the Federal Reserve, banking crises were not random, either from a cyclical or a seasonal perspective. All banking panics of the pre-Federal Reserve era occurred at seasonal loan-demand peaks (spring and fall)[3] that were also near business cycle peaks (Calomiris and Gorton 1991). At moments of high seasonal demand for lending, banks were relatively highly leveraged and had larger than normal loan-to-asset ratios, both of which implied higher risks of insolvency and illiquidity. With respect to cyclical timing, the panics before the Federal Reserve occurred whenever the quarterly (seasonally adjusted) liabilities of failed businesses equaled or exceeded 50 percent and the decline is stock prices equaled or exceeded about 8 percent. As contemporary observers recognized, banking panics in the United States were the result of the coincidence of sufficiently bad news about bank loan quality with sufficient bank balance sheet exposure to the insolvency and illiquidity risks implied by those prospective losses (seasonal highs in leverage and loan-to-asset ratios).

The National Monetary Commission — which was charged with developing a response to the problem of banking panics in the United States — commissioned studies of the banking system in the United States and other countries. Those clearly documented the greater instability of U.S. banking and specifically pointed to the fragmented nature of the United States' "unit" (single-office) banking system as a contributor to its vulnerability to cyclical and seasonal

---

[2] Calomiris and Gorton (1991) define six major panics that were large enough to generate information externalities and sufficient to motivate discussion of collective action by members of the New York Clearing House. Three of those six major banking crises (in 1873, 1893, and 1907) saw widespread suspension of the convertibility of deposits; the other three (in 1884, 1890, and 1896) saw banks contemplating or engaging in collective action to prevent potential suspension.

[3] See Hanes and Rhode (2013) for an analysis of the crop cycles that accounted for the seasonal pattern of loan demand in the United States during this period.

variation.[4] But the Commission knew that the fragmented U.S. banking structure was politically untouchable. The Commission did, however, believe that it was possible to reduce at least some of the liquidity risk that resulted from seasonal swings in loan demand, and this became a central motivation for the establishment of the Federal Reserve System.

As envisioned by the Federal Reserve's founders, the Federal Reserve Banks would be reservoirs of member bank reserves during times of low demand for loans and money and a source of additional reserves (via either lending to members or buying assets from them) during periods of high demand for credit and currency. The option to borrow would flatten the loan-supply function at times of seasonal stress, resulting both in lowered liquidity risk and less of a seasonal swing in interest rates.[5]

Before founding the Federal Reserve, there was good reason to believe that the proposed Federal Reserve System would reduce liquidity risk and prevent disruptions of the financial system. The shocks that triggered panics before the Federal Reserve was established were moderate compared, for example, to the shocks suffered from 1837-1839 or to later shocks during the 1930s. Panics spread because of uncertainty about banks' exposure to shocks that could undermine individual institutions but not threaten the solvency of the aggregate financial

---

[4] For example, Canada, which was the subject of three National Monetary Commission volumes, was also an agricultural economy and displayed high variation in seasonal loan demand. But its system of nationwide banks managed cyclical and seasonal risks without ever suffering a panic (Bordo et al. 2014, Calomiris and Haber 2014, Chapter 9). Canadian banks were better diversified, so there was less opportunity for moderate shocks to threaten the solvency of a major bank. Because Canadian banks operated nationwide networks of branches their western (agricultural) branches did not suffer the same seasonal liquidity risks of western and southern banks in the United States. Finally, in Canada, when concerns about uncertainty of bank losses arose, the small number of nationwide banks was able to manage the uncertainty by coordinating actions (including two selective bailouts via the collective acquisition of the failed banks, orchestrated by the Bank of Montreal) to stem depositors' concerns. In the United States, agricultural banks had to rely on interbank networks of distant banks to provide liquidity, and when systemic problems arose, it was virtually impossible to coordinate the resolution of the liquidity problems of separate banks across vast distances.

[5] In the presence of the Federal Reserve, banks have a new means other than recapitalization or loan liquidation to react to shocks that raise liquidity risk. The banking system avoids magnifying loan loss risk by creating a scramble for liquidating assets at a time of high leverage. The flattening of the loan-supply function means that variation in loan demand, seasonally or cyclically, should result in greater variation in the quantity of lending and lower variation in interest rates.

system. Although interest rates spiked and the payment system froze, few banks failed, and losses to creditors were small. The Panic of 1893 saw much worse depositor losses, which were roughly 0.10 percent of U.S. gross domestic product, or GDP. The depositor losses on average during each year of the Great Depression (1930-1933) were several times larger.[6]

Empirical evidence shows the Federal Reserve accomplished the central mission of increasing the seasonal elasticity of money and credit. Miron (1986) showed that the Federal Reserve's founding was associated with reduced seasonal variability of interest rates and increased seasonal variability of lending.[7] Bernstein et al. (2010) provide additional evidence that the Federal Reserve reduced seasonal liquidity risk. They compare the standard deviations of stock returns and short-term interest rates over time in the months of September and October (the two months of the year when markets were most vulnerable to a crash because of financial stringency from the harvest season) with the rest of the year before and after the establishment of the Federal Reserve. Stock volatility in those two months fell more than 40 percent and interest rate volatility more than 70 percent after the founding of the Federal Reserve. They also show this result was driven by years in which *business cycles peaked*. In other words, the main risk the Federal Reserve's founding eliminated was associated with combined cyclical peaks in economic

---

[6] The 9,096 banks that failed from 1930 through 1933 represented 37 percent of the banks in existence at the end of 1929 and 14 percent of the average level of bank deposits over the years 1930–1933. Losses borne by depositors in these failed banks were roughly $1.3 billion, representing 2.7 percent of the average amount of deposits in the banking system for the years 1930–1933, and 2 percent of average annual gross national product (GNP) for 1930–1933. (Deposits and failures data are from the Federal Reserve Board's data in Banking and Monetary Statistics: 1914–1941 (1943), using suspensions as the measures of failures. Nominal GNP is from the U.S. Department of Commerce's *Historical Statistics of the United States*, Vol. I, 1970.) In light of these comparatively large losses, it is not surprising that the Federal Reserve was unable to prevent panics or massive bank failures during the Great Depression, many of which occurred in agricultural areas experiencing severe adverse loan losses. Of course, the worst macroeconomic shocks of the Depression reflected errors of monetary policy, which were themselves a product of the Federal Reserve. There is evidence the Federal Reserve could have done more than it did to combat liquidity risk during the 1930s (see Richardson and Troost 2009, and Carlson, Mitchener and Richardson 2014).
[7] For additional evidence relating to expectations and the term structure of interest rates, see Mankiw and Miron (1987).

activity and seasonal peaks in lending — precisely the circumstances that had given rise to the panics of the pre-Federal Reserve era.

Despite this success, the Federal Reserve was unable to accomplish some of the major objectives envisioned by its founders, namely, universal bank membership in the Federal Reserve and the elimination of interbank deposits and reserve pyramiding in New York City. The use of interbank deposits as bank reserves continued after the founding of the Federal Reserve, because of features that limited state-chartered banks' interest in joining the Federal Reserve. These disincentives included the fact that the Federal Reserve did not pay interest on bank deposits, unlike money-center commercial banks in New York, Chicago, and elsewhere that paid about 2 percent. In many states, the Federal Reserve also required higher reserve requirements than those imposed by state governments on nonmember banks. Further discouraging state banks from joining the Federal Reserve was the fact that nonmember banks could indirectly benefit from the existence of the Federal Reserve without joining. Nonmember banks were able to access the Federal Reserve's discount window by passing their eligible paper through correspondent banks operating in reserve and central-reserve cities.

This paper looks at why many state-chartered banks chose not to join the Federal Reserve during the first decade of the Federal Reserve's operation, and in particular, why some joined immediately but others waited several years. To our knowledge, there has been no microeconometric analysis of the causes and consequences of state-chartered banks' decisions to join or not join the Federal Reserve System. This paper provides such analysis, focusing on the decisions of state-chartered New York banks from 1915 to 1924.

We investigate whether and how banks whose characteristics differed in important ways (specifically with respect to banks' exposures to liquidity risk, as well as their sizes, locations, and lending niches) had different propensities to join the Federal Reserve. Our empirical model identifies the extent to which banks differed with respect to the value of Federal Reserve membership. For example, we examine whether banks whose borrowers experienced high variation in seasonal loan demand anticipated benefits of liquidity risk reduction from joining the Federal Reserve. We find that the banks with high loan-demand seasonality, which presumably stood to gain the most from joining the Federal Reserve, joined earlier than others.

We also investigate how differences in banks' positions within the correspondent network affected their decisions to join the Federal Reserve. Some banks, by virtue of their size and geographic location, were positioned to be able to get easier access to the pass through of Federal Reserve liquidity without having to join the Federal Reserve. In those cases, small banks operating in close proximity to many Federal Reserve member banks should have been less likely to join the Federal Reserve, all things being equal, because they were able to gain easy indirect access to the Federal Reserve's discount window. Conversely, large banks that occupied important positions in the interbank network as takers of deposits should have seen Federal Reserve membership as particularly valuable means of attracting the deposits of nonmember banks and should have been among the first to join the Federal Reserve. Our empirical analysis supports all of these hypotheses.

With respect to the consequences of chartering the Federal Reserve, we are able to measure the extent to which member banks used the Federal Reserve's facilities to meet their liquidity needs. We examine the changes in lending activities of banks, before and after the creation of the Federal Reserve, both for Federal Reserve members and nonmembers. In doing so, we are able to distinguish between the advantages of operating in a banking system that included the Federal Reserve from the advantage of actually joining. We find that non-Federal

Reserve members were not able to enjoy all the benefits of access to the Federal Reserve's discount window, as members saw greater increases in lending. Clearly, there were limits to the benefits a nonmember could obtain through indirect access to the discount window. In particular, we consider whether practical constraints limited the ability of member banks to pass through the benefits of access to the discount window. For example, we investigate whether a small nonmember bank located in a city populated by many large Federal Reserve member banks was able to enjoy greater pass through benefits than a large nonmember bank (with larger rediscounting needs) located far from member banks.

The remainder of the paper is organized as follows. In Section 2, we review the details of the regulatory environment at the time of the Federal Reserve's founding with special emphasis on regulatory differences between the New York state banks that chose to join the Federal Reserve and those that did not. Section 3 describes in detail the data used in this study. Sections 4 and 5 present the empirical findings, which we divide into discussions of the determinants of membership (Section 4) and its consequences (Section 5). Section 6 concludes.

2. Dual Banking, Federal Reserve Membership, and the Federal Reserve's Early Years

A dual banking system of state-chartered banks and national banks characterized the U.S. banking system after the National Banking Acts of 1863 and 1864. By the time of the Federal Reserve Act, state-chartered and national banks had developed interconnected networks of banks operating throughout the country. Although banks in most states could not branch outside their local area, their networks linked banks across states through the correspondent network through which banks deposited reserves in each other and borrowed from one another.

State banks and trust companies were regulated by state legislatures. These institutions generally had lower minimum capital and minimum reserve ratio requirements than national banks, but did not issue bank notes due to a prohibitive tax of 10 percent per year on their outstanding bank notes. National banks were regulated by the Comptroller of the Currency. These banks had relatively high requirements and could issue national bank notes (subject to holding Treasury securities as backing) but could not issue mortgage loans.[8]

The National Monetary Commission's final report focused on flaws in the dual-banking system. The letter transmitting the final report to Congress summarized 17 "principal defects in our banking system (National Monetary Commission 1912 p. 6)." Thirteen of the 17 defects related to what economists now refer to as liquidity risk.[9] The Commission also highlighted the fragmented and inefficient U.S. banking system. The nation lacked efficient means of routing payments — particularly checks — from one region to another and for accommodating large, seasonal flows of funds between regions. Clearing checks could be slow and expensive. Many institutions charged fees for checks sent through the clearing system. These exchange charges provided substantial streams of revenue for many banks, particularly those operating in small towns and rural areas.

The Commission analyzed how banks could obtain liquidity. Banks had two options, but both were limited. First, they could obtain funds through membership at a nearby clearinghouse. Private clearinghouses, however, were limited to individual cities, and only extended liquidity to

---

[8] Calomiris and Carlson (2014) show that national banks were able to issue substantial amounts of mortgage loans despite the prohibition by taking mortgages as secondary collateral after loan origination.

[9] The first defect was immobility of cash reserves in times of trouble. The fifth was the lack of an organization larger than a city clearinghouse which could coordinate actions "to prevent panics or avert calamitous disturbances affecting the country at large." The sixth and seventh related to the lack of a lender of last resort which could shift reserves from one state to another to prevent "disastrous disruptions" of the payments system, or deal effectively with international gold and currency flows during financial crises. The eighth through twelfth pointed to the illiquidity of financial assets, particularly short-term commercial paper, during periods of seasonal strain or financial crises. All of these points related to liquidity risks posed by periods when commercial banks could not access reserves, sell assets, cooperate effectively, counteract interregional or international flows, or rely on a lender of last resort. Some of those institutional flaws also prevented banks from meeting normal or unusual seasonal demands for cash and credit. This problem was the focus of the Commission's third and fourth points (as well as points eight through fourteen), which described the inelasticity of the money supply, reflected in the lack of money supply variation in response to seasonal expansions and contractions of the economy.

members through the collective issuance of debt during panics (Cannon 1910, Timberlake 1984, Gorton 1985). Second, they could obtain funds from each other either through the sale of assets or via the correspondent network — that is, by withdrawing interbank deposits or by borrowing from one another. The National Banking Acts required national banks to hold a substantial fraction of their reserves in defined reserve and central reserve cities.[10] Because the pyramid structure concentrated money in financial centers, it magnified the extent to which regional and seasonal shocks spilled over to affect the entire country.

Liquidity provision was linked to the payments system. Clearinghouses cleared members' checks and held balances from members to facilitate these transactions. This ongoing relationship provided the foundation for the extension of credit during times of seasonal or cyclical stress. Similarly, correspondent networks' primary function was clearing checks, but these relationships also provided the foundation for the extension of credit during times of stress. Respondent banks (typically small, country banks) deposited funds in correspondents in reserve and central reserve cities. These deposits served as part of their legal reserves, received interest (typically 2 percent), and enabled respondents to deposit checks for clearing.

The Federal Reserve was created to solve the problems identified by the National Monetary Commission. The Federal Reserve would operate a nationwide and more efficient payments system, as well as create an elastic currency, a market for banks' eligible assets, a money supply that expanded at seasonal peaks, and a lender of last resort. The designers hoped to create a universal system, but bowed to political realities. National banks were the only bank

---

[10] Country national banks had to hold a reserve of 15 percent, of which three-fifths could be on deposit in a reserve city or central reserve city national bank. Reserve city national banks had to hold a reserve of 25 percent but again could deposit three-fifths in a central reserve city. Finally, central reserve cities had to hold a 25 percent reserve in vault cash. County banks were also required to redeem their notes at par in a reserve city and reserve city banks were required to redeem their notes in a central reserve city. Calomiris, Carlson, Jaremski, and Park (2014) find that in the 1890s national banks in the West and South held much more of their interbank deposits in New York City than did state-chartered banks, which held the vast majority of their reserves within their local regions.

type that could be required to join the Federal Reserve. State-chartered banks and trust companies were permitted, but not required, to join.[11] To join the Federal Reserve, state-chartered banks and trusts had to subject themselves to Federal Reserve regulatory requirements, most notably minimum bank size (capital) requirements (not to be confused with minimum capital ratio requirements), zero-interest reserve requirements, purchase stock in the Federal Reserve Bank, and other regulations, such as the requirement that member banks clear checks at par.

The Federal Reserve Board, however, expressed hope that it would develop a unified system of banking:

> In this process of developing the reserve power, of cultivating good relations with member banks, of educating their members to a recognition of the true theory upon which the reserve system is founded, and of otherwise carrying on the larger purposes aimed at by the Federal Reserve Act, the Board has been mindful of the delicate and important duty of unifying, so far as possible, the banking system of the country—a duty plainly imposed upon it by the provisions of the statute (1915, p. 11).

Despite that stated desire, state banks were slow to join. As shown in Figure 1, only 37 of more than 8,500 state-chartered banks joined the Federal Reserve by the end of 1916. The number of state-chartered bank members grew during the next year, but it was not until 1918 that entry became substantial. The number of state bank members grew to 938 members by the end of 1918 and 1,486 by 1920.

Why did so few state-chartered banks join the Federal Reserve after it began operations in November 1914? First, there were short-term operational problems at the time of the Federal Reserve's founding. World War 1 and the ensuing financial panic forced the Federal Reserve to begin operations months earlier than anticipated, under wartime conditions, and before the Federal Reserve had a chance to establish a check-clearing system. This exigency led to a

---

[11] The requirement of membership for national banks was hotly contested. The *Annual Report* of the Federal Reserve Board (1915, p. 12) describes two lawsuits challenging the constitutionality of section 11 (k).

prolonged period of initial adjustment, as the Federal Reserve struggled to get operations up to speed and the federal government imposed various wartime tasks upon the Federal Reserve. During this shake-out period, most state banks adopted a wait-and-see approach, trying to judge the benefits versus the costs of membership and remaining unwilling to expend the fixed costs of membership.

Second, during World War I, another major attraction of Federal Reserve membership — access to the discount window — was not reserved only for Federal Reserve members. Congress amended the Federal Reserve Act to compel the Reserve Banks to accept war bonds as collateral for discount loans and enable nonmember banks to borrow directly from the discount window.[12] After the war, member banks were given exclusive access to the discount window, as originally envisioned. The Federal Reserve Board also tried to block nonmembers from indirectly accessing the window by prohibiting member banks from bringing loans to the window that had been originated by nonmember institutions.

The Federal Reserve's check clearing rules may have reduced banks' gains from membership initially, but by early 1917, the Federal Reserve had successfully forced all New York banks — members and nonmembers alike — to clear checks at par, removing the cost of adhering to par check clearing regulation from the list of potential influences on the membership decision.[13] The Federal Reserve forced banks to join the par system by holding all checks drawn

---

[12]During World War 1, it was also the case that the seasonality of lending diminished because of the issuance of war loans and contracts (foreign and domestic) and because of the rationing and price controls imposed by the federal government. This also temporarily diminished the attractiveness of Federal Reserve membership.

[13] The Federal Reserve's founders envisioned the creation of a universal par check-clearing system. The Federal Reserve would absorb clearinghouses in the cities where it operated and would clear checks for all banks in the nation. The checks would clear at face value. Banks would not be permitted to deduct fees from checks routed through clearinghouses or the mail, rather than presented at their counter. These exchange charges, however, were a substantial source of revenue for many state-chartered banks. Those banks did not want to forgo this profitable activity. In the Federal Reserve's early years, it seemed as if they would not have to. Several banks in Manhattan, including the Guaranty Trust Company, offered to establish clearing accounts for country clients, pay 2 percent interest on the balances, and allow exchange charges. The Federal Reserve countered these plans, eventually promising to clear all checks for free,

on nonpar institutions for several months. After accumulating checks worth substantial sums, the Federal Reserve sent an agent to present those checks at the banks' counters, where they had to be cleared immediately in cash at face value. This practice forced nonpar banks to keep large sums of cash in their vaults. By July 1917, all banks in the district had joined the par list, eliminating exchange charges as a reason to eschew Federal Reserve membership. Other Federal Reserve banks behaved similarly throughout the United States.

The Federal Reserve's zero-interest reserve requirements were viewed as one of the primary factors in banks' membership choices. Requirements were loosened by an amendment to the Federal Reserve Act passed in June of 1917, but remained costly for many banks in comparison to the zero-interest reserve requirement costs for nonmember banks. The 1917 Amendment required member banks to hold all required reserves at the Federal Reserve, rather than only a fraction of required reserves under the previous requirements (see Table 1). At the same time, the 1917 Amendment reduced the value of required reserves on demand deposits by 5 percentage points and on time deposits by 2 percentage points across all banks. The 1917 Amendment also codified the Federal Reserve's administrative regulations concerning state bank members. Although the Board states the section was "practically an enactment of the Board's regulations on that subject already in effect," they hoped it would properly assure state banks that there would be "no interference with its charter and statutory rights, and that it may continue to exercise all powers granted to it under such charter" (1917, p. 502).

Although membership increased a bit after 1917, Federal Reserve membership remained far from universal. As Figure 1 shows, even at its height, membership represented only a third of all the commercial banks in the nation and less than 8 percent of banks that had the choice to

---

establishing programs to teach banks how to structure their fees to make up for lost exchange charges, and creating national and district par lists. The par lists indicated all banks that had agreed to forgo exchange charges, whether members of the system or not.

join. The participation rate was particularly low for small country banks in agricultural regions. A joint Congressional Committee was organized in 1920 to investigate the low adoption rate. The committee identified three major reasons for the behavior.[14] First, (as White 1983 would later echo), in spite of Federal Reserve efforts to limit indirect access to the discount window by nonmembers, banks were able to circumvent those limits and access cash related to their seasonal or cyclical needs through correspondent banks that were members of the Federal Reserve System, escaping the burdens of actual membership. Second, by keeping their reserves at a correspondent bank that paid interest rather than the Federal Reserve Banks that paid nothing, banks could turn a profit from reserves. Finally, the returns to stock investments in the Federal Reserve were not considered remunerative enough to induce small banks to join.

Table 1 presents the requirements facing Federal Reserve state member banks (state banks and trust companies that voluntarily subjected themselves to the Federal Reserve's requirements) and nonmember New York state banks (state banks and trust companies that were under the state's requirements) in 1915 before the Amendment of 1917. Minimum capital requirements were somewhat higher for state member banks in larger cities, but the constraint most often did not bind in those cities because of the economic advantages of larger bank size.

The most important discrepancy between the two sets of regulations seems to have been reserve requirements. For starters, state nonmember banks were required to hold deposits only against demand deposits, but state member banks were required to hold deposits against demand *and* time deposits. Member banks also were required to deposit reserves with the Federal Reserve instead of allowing them to be deposited with a qualified correspondent (typically earning 2 percent interest rather than zero).

---

[14] *Congressional Quarterly* (1923). To a lesser degree, the committee also concluded that the lack of adoption might also have been influenced by the fear of changes in the attitude or regulations of the Federal Reserve Board.

The amount of required reserves for state member banks was generally lower than those for nonmember state-chartered banks in New York, but the amount of zero-interest reserves (the sum of required cash on hand plus reserves held at the Federal Reserve) generally was higher for member banks. For example, for a bank operating in a nonreserve city (such as Rochester) with $1 million in demand deposits and $200,000 in time deposits, its total zero-interest required reserves as a Federal Reserve member would have been

$$(0.12)(1.00)\$1,000,000 + (0.05)(1.00)\$200,000 = \$120,000 + \$10,000 = \$130,000.$$

For that same bank, its zero-interest required reserves as a nonmember bank would be

$$(0.15)(0.40)\$1,000,000 = \$60,000.$$

For a similarly situated bank in a reserve city (either Albany or Brooklyn before 1917, with the addition of Buffalo in that year), its zero-interest required reserves as a Federal Reserve member would have been

$$(0.15)(1.00)\$1,000,000 + (0.05)(1.00)\$200,000 = \$160,000$$

but as a nonmember its zero-interest required reserves would again be $60,000.

For that same bank operating in Manhattan (the only central reserve city), Federal Reserve membership would require it to hold zero-interest reserves equal to

$$(0.18)(1.00)\$1,000,000 + (0.05)(1.00)\$200,000 = \$180,000 + \$10,000 = \$190,000$$

compared to

$$(0.25)(0.60)\$1,000,000 = \$150,000$$

if it were a nonmember bank. For most banks in New York, with the important exception of banks located in New York City, reserve requirements as members of the Federal Reserve were much more costly than those required by the state. In New York City, Federal Reserve zero-interest reserve requirements were greater, but not dramatically so.

14

The Amendment of 1917 lowered the zero-interest required reserves of banks — which presumably helped to spur the growth of membership from 1918 to 1920, shown in Figure 1— for most New York state-chartered banks located outside New York City. However, the Federal Reserve's rules on zero-interest required reserves were still significantly more costly than the rules for nonmember banks. For example, for the bank operating in Albany, its zero-interest required reserves as a Federal Reserve member bank were now

$$(0.10)\$1,000,000 + (0.03)\$200,000 = \$106,000$$

which is still substantially greater than the $60,000 zero-interest reserve it was required to maintain as a nonmember bank.

As a simple test of the importance of zero-interest reserve requirements in discouraging Federal Reserve membership, we estimated the amount in saved zero-interest required reserves relative to assets that each New York state bank stood to gain from not becoming a Federal Reserve member in 1917 (before the Amendment) and in 1920. We define *ResReqGain* as the difference between the amount of zero-interest required reserves a subject bank would have to hold as a Federal Reserve member and what it would have to hold as a nonmember (note that for some banks, such as those in New York City after 1917, this could be a negative number). We then compute the estimated amount of *ResReqGain* as a fraction of total assets for each bank, *ResReqGain/Assets*.[15] Finally, we compute the average of *ResReqGain/Assets* for member banks and nonmember banks. We find that the average value of that ratio for banks that had joined the Federal Reserve by 1917 is 2.21 percent, compared to 4 percent for banks that had not joined the Federal Reserve by that date. After 1917, *ResReqGain/Assets* declined for all banks as a consequence of the Amendment. The average value for banks that had joined the Federal

---

[15] To compute *ResReqGain* we must impute total amounts of time and demand deposits for each bank. Bank records of individual banks only give total deposits, so we used the state-level aggregate amounts of time and demand deposits to estimate the amount of each for each bank.

Reserve by 1920 is -1.15 percent, compared to 0.86 percent for banks that had not yet joined the Federal Reserve.[16] Clearly, on average, the banks that chose to remain outside the Federal Reserve stood to lose more from Federal Reserve requirements that forced them to hold zero-interest reserves than the banks that chose to join the Federal Reserve. The Amendment of 1917 reversed the relative costliness of reserve requirements for some banks, many of which chose to join the Federal Reserve. The effect on state-chartered banks in New York City was relatively strong. In New York City, 62 percent of state banks had joined the Federal Reserve by 1920 (up from 2.7 percent in 1916), compared with only 23 percent of state banks outside New York City (up from zero in 1916).

Although the cost of the Federal Reserve's requirements was clearly a major contributor to state banks' reluctance to join, it was only one side of banks' cost-benefit analysis. Much of the variation in membership choice remains to be explained, both within the group of banks operating outside of New York City and within New York City banks. Presumably, that variation in membership choice within groups of banks that faced similar reserve requirement tradeoffs largely reflected bank-specific differences in the benefits of Federal Reserve membership.[17] We explore those in Section 4.

3. Data

We construct a new database containing the balance sheet items of each state bank and trust company in New York from 1912 to 1924. Balance sheets for all state banks and trust companies

---

[16] The values for 1918 and 1919 are nearly identical to those for 1920.

[17] We recognize, of course, that the costliness of reserve requirements may also have varied within the bank groups as a consequence of their lending opportunities: Banks with more profitable lending opportunities would have found zero-interest reserve requirements more of a burden. Consistent with that view, as shown in Table 2, banks that were among the first to join the Federal Reserve (by 1915) tended to have lower loan-to-asset ratios in 1914 than those that chose not to join the Federal Reserve.

were published every year by the State of New York Banking Department, which conducted inspections of all financial intermediaries that held a state charter. The resulting information was published in the *Annual Report of the Superintendent of Banks*. To avoid potential endogeneity problems relating to entry in reaction to changes in regulation during our sample period, we limit the sample to the 190 banks and 77 trust companies that were present before the Federal Reserve was created.

There are clear reasons for focusing the analysis on a single state. The costs and benefits of Federal Reserve membership likely depended upon regulations under which state-chartered banks operated. For example, in places where state banks faced lower reserve requirements, the decision to become a Federal Reserve member would have been more costly. Focusing on one state avoids complications in the estimation of parameters that arise from multiple state-level regulatory regimes, particularly when unobserved heterogeneity in economic conditions could be correlated both with state regulations and economic outcomes.

Given the advantages of focusing on a single state, studying New York has several advantages. First, New York state-chartered banks are sufficiently numerous, and the state's bank records are rich and accessible. Furthermore, banking in New York is diverse enough — as reflected in the variety of bank sizes, lending functions, and locations — to permit one to identify the full range of bank attributes likely to have mattered for understanding how different banks' circumstances affected state-chartered banks' decisions to join the Federal Reserve and the consequences of those decisions.

Second, the state-chartered banks in New York are largely representative of the banking system throughout the United States. New York contained all three layers of the reserve pyramid: country, reserve, and central reserve; a feature shared with only one other state. Our analysis indicates that banks in these layers responded differently to the creation of the Federal Reserve. This observation could not be made when studying most other states. Moreover, New York prohibited banks from branching outside their home towns, meaning that a large number of small banks served depositors and borrowers who lived in their vicinity. These country banks in turn held reserves at larger banks, generally Federal Reserve members after 1914, in what would eventually be the reserve cities of Albany, Brooklyn, Buffalo, and the Bronx, and the central reserve city of New York.

Third, New York was the financial center in the United States, holding an average of over 40 percent of U.S. bank assets between 1912 and 1924. A change in the state's banks and trust companies thus represented a large change in the system as a whole.

Fourth, the state's wide range of economic and demographic areas provides sufficient sample size and variation to study all types of areas. The state was home to the metropolis of New York City, medium-sized cities with active manufacturing and industrial bases, and many small towns in rural and agricultural areas.

Fifth, the correspondent network of New York is more accurately estimated than the networks of the other states. Lacking information on the specific balances that each bank kept at other banks, most studies use the list of correspondents drawn from the various bank directories of the times. Although listed banks were almost always accurate, the directories tended to list New York City banks ahead of others and often could not include all correspondents due to space constraints, which biases the picture of interbank networks in most states. For example, in the case of Illinois, where the preservation of state examination reports permits us to examine correspondent balances, banks kept the majority of funds in the nearest reserve city. However, this problem does not arise for New York state. Because New York was the nearest reserve city

18

for all banks in the state, bank directories should generally provide a complete picture of the structure of New York banks' correspondent relationships.

The potential disadvantage of New York state is that New York City banks had different opportunities and regulations relative to other banks. Any analysis of New York banks' behavior must take into account those differences. As a central reserve city, the city's banks became home to the vast majority of the nation's interbank deposits. The city's securities markets also could have yielded different portfolios than banks in other states. To capture these important differences, we employ location-specific controls in some specifications, and in others, we split the sample to distinguish between those located in and outside New York City.

We consult the *Annual Report of the Federal Reserve Board* to determine whether a bank was a member of the Federal Reserve. The report contains a list of all state member banks by district each year. We then matched these lists to the balance sheet data, creating a dummy variable for whether the bank was a member in the given year. Figure 2 presents a map showing the locations of the 81 of 267 state-chartered institutions in the sample that joined the Federal Reserve system by 1924. The figure also shows that state member banks were spread out across the state, but were particularly attracted to the population centers along transportation lines. The line of members running east-west across the middle of the state and down the east side follows the old Erie Canal and the railroads that later replaced it. Figure 3 displays the timing of new Federal Reserve members by year and location, showing that membership became more geographically dispersed over time.

We augment the state bank and trust company data in a variety of ways. First, we document the location of each bank's correspondents as listed in *the Rand McNally* or *Polk's Bankers Directories*. We document these in 1913, 1915, 1917, and 1920 and fill any data gaps with the preceding value. Second, we document whether the bank was a member of the local clearinghouse using the same two directories. Third, we obtain the location and balance sheet information of all national banks from Jaremski (2013). Finally, we add county-level Census information for 1920 from the database assembled by Haines (2004). Although we could have used values in 1910, the Census for that year did not tabulate manufacturing data, which is our reason for using later values.

4. Explaining Membership Choices of State-Chartered Banks

Section 2 reviewed how the costs and benefits of joining the Federal Reserve varied during its first decade, as the Federal Reserve altered policies to aid the war effort and promote membership. Key changes occurred in 1917, when the Federal Reserve imposed the par clearing system and lowered member bank reserve requirements, and at the end of the war, when the Federal Reserve closed the discount window to nonmembers and adopted policies that impeded correspondents from discounting paper originated by nonmember banks. The costs and benefits of membership also varied across banks with different characteristics, including location. It is important that any model of Federal Reserve membership choice take account of differences across time, location, and bank circumstances.

The first prominent explanation for joining the Federal Reserve is that membership gave banks access to seasonal liquidity. We measure the seasonal demand for liquidity using the average percent change in loans between the third and fourth quarters across 1912, 1913, and 1914.[18] The benefit of access to Federal Reserve liquidity, however, might have been smaller for banks that had alternative means of accessing liquidity. Banks could obtain liquidity from New

---

[18] Although unreported, we find similar results using other measures of loan variations, such as the standard deviation of loans over four quarters and the average percent change in loans between the first and fourth quarters.

York City correspondents, from correspondents in reserve cities or local towns, or by selling instruments such as banker's acceptances in the open market. Banks that had access to these options may have been less likely to join the Federal Reserve. We control for whether the bank was a member of the local clearinghouse and the share of a bank's correspondents in Manhattan to determine the extent that the bank could receive liquidity through existing relationships, as well as the amount of assets in local Federal Reserve banks and the relative size of the bank to capture a bank's ability to sell acceptances through the secondary market. Note that clearinghouses also offered a source of liquidity, which might have reduced the benefits of Federal Reserve membership, making clearinghouse members less likely to join the Federal Reserve. But throughout the United States and in New York particularly, clearinghouses supported the creation of the Federal Reserve and urged members to join, and in New York City, eventually transferred many of their functions to the Federal Reserve Banks.

A major part of the attraction of Federal Reserve membership to clearinghouse members in New York City and other money centers was that Federal Reserve membership enhanced the role that these banks could play as nodes in the correspondent network. They may have seen *greater* advantages from joining the Federal Reserve, in particular if they were able to act as intermediaries channeling the benefits of access to the Federal Reserve's discount window to nonmember country banks. It is important to consider how a bank's position as a "due-to" intermediary of interbank deposits (that is, a bank receiving substantial deposits from other banks) affected its decision about Federal Reserve membership. A high proportion of due-to balances was highly correlated with clearinghouse membership in cities outside New York City and with large "due-from" positions in New York City.

In light of these considerations about how the correspondent network affected banks incentives to provide or receive pass-throughs of discount window access, we devote considerable attention to determining each bank's position in New York's correspondent network. As Figure 4 shows, as of 1915, correspondent banks were almost exclusively located in a handful of important cities in New York. Figure 5 shows the structure of the interbank network as of 1920. Virtually all banks had a correspondent relationship with one or more banks in New York City (Panel A). In other significant New York cities (Albany, Buffalo, Rochester, Syracuse, and Troy) a hub and spoke pattern is visible, where due-to banks had correspondents within their regions. In some other cities, due-to banks had one or two correspondent relationships with nearby banks.

We measure the extent that a bank was a correspondent using a variety of different measures. First, we create an indicator variable denoting whether the bank was listed as a correspondent of another bank in the state.[19] Second, we include the number of correspondents a bank listed in the bank directories. Third, we include a trust company indicator to control for the different type of corporate structure and investment strategy. Amongst state-chartered institutions, trust companies not only were large but they also attracted a large number of interbank deposits and were themselves major depositors in other banks. Fourth, we include a clearinghouse membership indicator to control for the extent of existing interbank clearing relationships. Because clearinghouses provided emergency liquidity and check clearing services, clearinghouse banks often attracted more interbank deposits than other banks. The clearinghouse variable captures opposing influences. If being a clearinghouse member makes banks more likely to adopt Federal Reserve membership, then interbank networks for discount window "pass-

---

[19] Even though the results are similar using the number of times a bank was listed as a correspondent, we have chosen to use a dummy variable because we do not have correspondent data for every bank in the United States.

through" were an important consideration. Alternatively, if clearinghouse membership makes banks less likely to adopt, that suggests a lesser role for pass-through, and the relative importance of access to emergency liquidity from the clearinghouse as a substitute for Federal Reserve membership.

While the discount window and correspondent network might be the more prominent explanations, there are many other factors that might have driven membership adoption which we take into account. The capacity of a bank to bear the fixed costs of becoming a Federal Reserve member also plays a role in its decision. While New York state regulations were among the most stringent in the country, adoption of a membership still came with additional compliance costs. Large banks would have been better able to shoulder the additional compliance burden of Federal Reserve membership, implying that size in itself should be correlated with Federal Reserve membership. As noted, we must also control for location, which mattered for determining the costs of Federal Reserve reserve requirements. Locational factors also likely influenced the adoption rate for other reasons, such as differences in the opportunity cost of lending, the mix of deposits and reserve requirement costs, or local political factors that favored or discouraged membership.

4.1. Empirical Specifications

Modeling a bank's decision to become a Federal Reserve member is fraught with potential endogeneity problems. In particular, it is tempting to include balance sheet measures that might capture relevant factors relating to costs or benefits of membership (e.g., a bank's exogenous willingness to lend more should be correlated with the profitability of lending, which could signal the costliness of higher zero-interest reserve requirements), but those balance sheet ratios may respond to the prospect of Federal Reserve membership. We take several steps to minimize this endogeneity problem. First, as noted above, we examine only state banks and trust companies that existed in 1914. This removes institutions whose entry might have been influenced by the availability of Federal Reserve membership.[20] Second, with the exception of a relative asset variable, we use bank-specific balance sheet values from before 1915. Finally, our dependent variable is forward looking — whether the bank joined the Federal Reserve in the following year — and we drop observations after a bank became a Federal Reserve member in order to capture the membership decision and not changes made after the decision.[21]

Our base-line specification uses a log-logistic survival model to examine the determinants of joining the Federal Reserve for the period 1915-1920.[22] Each bank enters the model in 1915 and exits when it became a Federal Reserve member. The approach explicitly models the probability of becoming a member for each year using a log-logistic function and identifies the coefficients from those institutions that became members faster or slower than predicted. The model has the function of:

$$BecomeMember_{i,t} = fn\left(\beta_1 Z_{i,t} + \beta_2 X_{i,1920} + \beta_3 BS_{i,1912-14} + e_{i,t}\right) \quad (1)$$

where $BecomeMember_{i,t}$ is a dummy variable denoting whether the institution became a Federal Reserve member in the *subsequent* year. $Z_{i,t}$ is a vector of bank-specific characteristics. $X_{i,1920}$ is a vector of county-characteristics taken from the Census in 1920. $BS_{i,1912-14}$ is a

---

[20] For instance, several banks that entered after 1914 immediately adopted Federal Reserve membership.

[21] It is worth noting that all the banks in our sample that became Federal Reserve members remained Federal Reserve members for the remainder of our sample period. Only two banks in New York adopted and then dropped their membership in New York during the period. Neither of those banks existed in 1914 and so neither is in our sample.

[22] Although we have membership and balance sheet data through 1924, only one state bank in existence in 1914 became a Federal Reserve member between 1920 and 1924. Rather than attach excessive weight to this single observation, we drop the remaining years from the sample.

vector of balance sheet items from the pre-Federal Reserve era.[23] We estimate the model alternating between including the county-characteristics and county-fixed effects. While county-fixed effects offer the best control for local effects, their inclusion necessitates that we drop banks that were in a county where no banks chose to become Federal Reserve members before 1920.

In summary, the vector of characteristics included in our empirical estimation was chosen based on the factors described above, and include the following sets of characteristics:

Bank-specific characteristics — An indicator variable denoting whether the bank was a trust company, another denoting whether the bank was a clearinghouse member, the number of miles the bank was from a Federal Reserve district bank[24], the number of correspondents listed in the banker directories, the share of listed correspondents of the subject bank in Manhattan, an indicator variable denoting whether the bank was listed as correspondent of another bank, the logarithm of all Federal Reserve member banks' assets within 25 miles of the subject bank, and the ratio of the bank's assets to the assets of Federal Reserve member banks within 25 miles of the subject bank.

County-specific characteristics — To further capture aspects of location that may have affected the degree of bank isolation or the profitability of lending, we include the logarithm of population, the fraction of the population located in urban areas, the fraction that is illiterate, the logarithm of farm output per capita, the logarithm of manufacturing output per capita, the number of acres in cereal production, and the logarithm of the number of fruit trees, all of which were measured in 1920.

---

[23] The dates for the variables included in the $BS_{i,1912-14}$ vector vary. Assets are measured in 1914. Loans/assets and seasonal loan swing are averages for the period.

[24] We allow the distance to adjust when Buffalo gained a branch in 1919.

Balance-sheet characteristics — We include the logarithm of total assets in 1914, which should matter either because of the fixed costs of regulatory compliance, or through the relative ability of smaller banks to access local pass-throughs without joining the Federal Reserve. We also include the average ratio of loans to assets between 1912 and 1914. This variable could capture opposing influences on Federal Reserve membership. On the one hand, it may capture the extent to which lending is profitable and zero-interest reserve requirements of the Federal Reserve are a burden. From that perspective, one would expect a higher loan ratio to be a negative predictor of membership. Alternatively, the loan ratio could capture the extent to which the bank expects to benefit from liquidity risk reduction from obtaining access to the discount window, which would imply an opposite, positive coefficient. A more unambiguous measure of the benefits of Federal Reserve membership is the extent to which lending varies across seasons, which was an important source of systemic liquidity risk, as we noted in the introduction. We expect this measure of seasonality in lending to be positively associated with choosing to join the Federal Reserve. We measure the seasonality of loan demand as the absolute value of the average change between a bank's loans in the third and fourth quarters (the seasonal peak and trough of lending) in the years 1912 through 1914.[25]

In Table 3, we present three sets of specification. The first is a parsimonious specification that does not include indicator variables for whether the institution was a trust company or a clearinghouse member. That specification considers whether banks listed by other banks as correspondents tended to join the Federal Reserve relatively quickly. Because 25 of the 28 ("due-to") correspondent banks were either trust companies or clearinghouse members or both, we first drop the extra indicators for those attributes when considering whether due-to designation

---

[25] We could not go further back in time than 1912 because trust company data is not reported in the *Annual Report* before that date. The results are similar but smaller if we use the average percentage change in loans from the first quarter to the fourth quarter.

matters for Federal Reserve membership.[26] The second specification adds the trust company and

clearinghouse member indicators for comparison. The final specification adds the pre-1915

balance sheet characteristics.

As shown in Table 3, institutions that were listed as correspondents were much more

likely to become Federal Reserve members. The coefficient on due-to correspondents is only

statistically significant when the trust company and clearinghouse indicators are excluded

(reflecting the substantial overlap between these groups of banks). As noted before, trust

companies and clearinghouse members were among the most likely to be holding significant

interbank deposits, and it was these characteristics that likely encouraged early Federal Reserve

membership. In column (6) for instance, the effect of being a due to correspondent actually

increases the time it takes until membership by 31 percent, but being a trust company or a

clearinghouse member decreases it by 22 and 34 percent, respectively.[27] The effect of the bank's

location in the correspondent network played a significant role in determining the speed of

adoption.

We also find evidence that, in spite of Federal Reserve efforts to limit pass-throughs,

banks seeking to avoid the costs of Federal Reserve membership were able to obtain pass-

throughs of discount window access from surrounding Federal Reserve member banks. We find

that the composition, not the number, of a bank's due-from correspondents has a meaningful

effect on the decision to become a member. Banks that joined the Federal Reserve had fewer

Manhattan correspondents yet did not have significantly more total correspondents. In column

---

[26] We identify due-to banks as banks listed as correspondents by one or more state-chartered banks operating in New York state. We recognize that it is conceivable that some additional state-chartered banks in New York may only have been acting as due-to banks for banks outside of New York state, or only for national banks operating within New York. However, by limiting our analysis to state-chartered New York banks, we ensure that our identified due-to banks are playing an important role in the network in which New York's state-chartered banks are operating.

[27] We translate the coefficients into percentage change in time until membership using the following formula: $100[\exp(\beta)-1]$.

(6), each extra correspondent only increased the time until membership by 2.5 percent, yet each 25 percentage point increase in the Manhattan share (i.e., about one more Manhattan correspondent) slowed adoption by 12.5 percent. [28] Moreover, being surrounded by large Federal Reserve member banks discouraged banks from becoming members. A bank with a standard deviation more assets in surrounding Federal Reserve banks (2.44) took 53 percent longer to become a member. The coefficient for being around large Federal Reserve banks is only significant when including county-fixed effects that suggest banks in a county's largest city were the most likely to join the Federal Reserve. This finding matches the distribution of state bank members in New York state, because many counties only had one state-chartered member bank and it was not often located in the city with the largest national bank population. Overall, our results strongly support the proposition that nonmember banks used their Federal Reserve-member neighbors and correspondents as substitutes for joining the Federal Reserve.

When added to the model, a bank's size and its loan variation are significant determinants of membership. A large bank, or a bank with greater seasonal loan variation, was significantly more likely to become members even controlling for the bank's correspondent status. Using the county-fixed effect coefficients, a bank was 36.9 percent faster to adopt membership for every standard deviation increase in Assets (1.5), and was 5.7 percent faster for every standard deviation increase in loan swing (0.087). These findings support the view that banks that were large enough to absorb the compliance costs of Federal Reserve membership, but perhaps too large to rely on local Federal Reserve members for pass-through lending, found greater net value in Federal Reserve membership. The loan seasonality effect provides clear evidence that banks expected to gain advantages related to liquidity risk reduction from joining the Federal Reserve.

---

[28] Both values are actually close to being one standard deviation. The standard deviation of the number of correspondents is 1.35 and the standard deviation of the share of correspondents in Manhattan is 0.26.

4.2. Additional Specifications

Here we examine several additional specifications. Although including due-to correspondent banks expands our sample size and variation, and permits us to explore particular aspects of the correspondent network relevant for Federal Reserve membership choice, there are also advantages of restricting the sample to exclude these banks. As a result of their quick adoption, there are too few observations to study only the sample of due-to banks.

In Table 4, we drop the 28 banks listed as due-to correspondents from the sample and re-estimate the survival model.[29] Here we see that the results are very similar to those in Table 3, particularly for the model with bank fixed effects, although the levels of statistical significance are understandably a bit lower for the clearinghouse and trust company indicator variables.

Table 5 reports another robustness check. Here we drop all New York City banks from the sample to make sure that our results are not driven by unusual circumstances relating to New York City banks that were not due-to correspondents (which, like other New York City banks, operated under unique reserve requirement laws). Coefficient values are very similar to those in tables 3 and 4.

The results in tables 3 through 5 indicate that due-to correspondent banks adopted memberships for different reasons than noncorrespondent banks. Noncorrespondent banks often responded to their need for liquidity by accessing pass-throughs from surrounding Federal Reserve members, but correspondent banks (consisting almost entirely of trust companies and clearinghouse members) joined the Federal Reserve to expand their network.

---

[29] Note that we have to drop the distance to the nearest Federal Reserve city from the hazard due to lack of variation. We also cannot include county-fixed effects because all of the institutions are in the same county.

The estimates in tables 3 through 5 assume that coefficients on explanatory variables remained constant over time. Section 2 presented historical information, which suggests the influence of some of these variables may have varied over time. For example, banks whose Manhattan correspondents cleared checks for them may have been initially reluctant to join the Federal Reserve, since they would have lost the benefit of exchange charges and received no interest on large required reserves. These concerns probably eased after the Federal Reserve imposed par clearing in 1916 and eased reserve requirements in 1917. Banks whose lending exhibited large seasonal swings in peacetime may have had little incentive to join the Federal Reserve during the war, when war programs overrode seasonal cycles and the Federal Reserve opened its discount window to all banks holding war bonds — essentially all banks. To determine whether the impact of our explanatory variables changed over time, we estimate three separate logit regressions.

Each regression examines whether a bank adopted membership during the defined period given the value of the variables at the beginning of the period. We define these periods as 1915-16, 1917, and 1918-20, because during these periods, banks faced relatively stable costs and benefits, as discussed in Section 2[30] A positive coefficient implies the institution was more likely to become a member.

Table 6 shows how different factors mattered more or less at different times. Being a clearinghouse member mattered most during the early years of the Federal Reserve. This makes intuitive sense, because the New York Clearing House encouraged all of its members to join the Federal Reserve. The share of Manhattan correspondents also mattered in early years, when country banks continued to profit from exchange charges. This variable ceased to be important

---

[30] There were 28 adoptions in 1915/1916, 34 adoptions in 1917, and 11 adoptions in 1918/1919/1920.

after 1916, when the Federal Reserve imposed par clearing throughout New York state, when country banks ceased to earn exchange charges, and when the Federal Reserve eased reserve requirements for state-chartered banks. Large correspondent banks made their decisions about the Federal Reserve very quickly, but noncorrespondent banks made their decisions to join the Federal Reserve after 1917. Due to banks seem to have joined to grow their network, while other banks joined the Federal Reserve to mitigate the risks associated with large seasonal fluctuations in loan demand once the lay of the land in the due-to banks' decisions had already been made and the regulatory costs of Federal Reserve membership had declined sufficiently.

The raw data on the growth in the number of correspondent relationships of due-to banks confirms the role of Federal Reserve membership in promoting the growth of member banks' networks. This pattern is particularly visible outside New York City. In cities such as Albany, Buffalo, Rochester, Syracuse, and Troy, Federal Reserve member banks that already had correspondent banks in 1915 saw the average number of correspondents increase from 2.3 in 1915 to 3.8 in 1920. Only two nonmember member banks in those cities had any correspondents in 1915, and their average number of correspondents declined from 3 in 1915 to 2.8 by 1920. In those same locations, for member banks that had no correspondents in 1915, the number of correspondents in 1920 rose to roughly one for every eight Federal Reserve member banks. Within New York City, Federal Reserve member "due-to" banks also saw absolute and relative growth in their networks — increasing from an average of 6.3 correspondents in 1915 to an average of 8.5 in 1920. For nonmember banks in New York City, the average number of correspondents increased less, from 2.3 to 2.7.

Table 6 shows that the seasonality of a bank's lending, as measured by the seasonal swing in the three years preceding World War 1, was not correlated with decisions to join the

Federal Reserve in 1915, 1916, and 1917. The early insignificance of this coefficient likely reflects the combination of higher regulatory costs of membership, the low seasonality of lending during the war years, and the ability of nonmember banks to access the discount window during that time. These policies changed after the war, when the Federal Reserve ceased lending to nonmembers and adopted rules (fully implemented in 1919) attempting to prohibit the pass-through of eligible paper originated by nonmembers.

As a further robustness check, in Table 7 we estimate a logit regression where the dependent variable is whether the bank became a Federal Reserve member by 1920. The independent variables enter with their 1915 values. The results are similar (with opposite signs) to the previous survival models. The size of loan seasonal variation, value of assets, and share of nonManhattan correspondents consistently increase the probability of Federal Reserve membership. The effects of most other variables retain their direction but lose some statistical significance, which is not surprising given the loss in information associated with combining all the years rather than distinguishing among various timings of membership choice (as in tables 3 through 6) to gauge the relative strength of the subject bank's interest in membership.

5. The Consequences of Joining the Federal Reserve

The previous section analyzed the decision of state-chartered New York banks whether to become Federal Reserve members; in this section, we examine how membership changed banks' behavior over the sample period of 1915-1924.

We consider four measures of banks' behavior: the percentage seasonal swing in lending, the ratio of cash (defined as vault cash plus cash items) relative to total assets, the ratio of the amount due-from banks plus due-from the Federal Reserve relative to total assets, and loans relative to total assets. We consider changes in the levels of these because we expect membership

to be associated with a one-time level effect rather than a continuous change over time. For

instance, if the discount window eliminated all loan variation for members, the change in

variation would be negative for one period and close to zero every period thereafter.[31]

The model takes the form:

$$Y_{i,t} = a + \beta_1 MemberBy1924_i + \beta_2 Member_{i,t} + \beta_3 Z_{i,t} + \beta_4 X_{i,1920} + \beta_5 BS_{i,1912-14} + t_t$$
$$+ e_{i,t} \quad (2)$$

where $Y_{i,t}$ is any of the previously mentioned dependent variables, $MemberBy1924_i$ is an

indicator variable denoting whether the bank joined the Federal Reserve at any time before 1924,

$Member_{i,t}$ is a dummy variable denoting whether the bank was a member of the Federal Reserve

in that particular year, t_t is a vector of year fixed effects, and the rest of the variables retain their

previous definitions. The model measures whether the observed variables were higher or lower

after the bank joined the Federal Reserve. $MemberBy1924_i$ controls for constant differences

between institutions that joined the Federal Reserve and those that did not change across the

entire period, while $Member_{i,t}$ captures the specific effect that becoming a member had on the

institution. To further control for potential differences between banks, we separately estimate the

specification with the county-level variables or with bank fixed effects. The county-

characteristics model effectively looks at whether a bank changed relative to other banks *and*

relative to its own history (after controlling for county characteristics), while the bank-fixed

effects model effectively *only* looks at within-bank variation over time.

Table 8 shows that banks altered their behavior after becoming Federal Reserve

members. Membership decreased a bank's seasonal loan variation. A bank that became a

---

[31] We also find differences in rates of change in these dependent variables when we control for convergence effects with lagged levels of dependent variables.

member saw its loan swing *decrease* between 1.5 and 1.9 percent. The coefficient is larger when county-fixed effects are included, suggesting that the change is driven by within-bank change over time. It is also important to note that the average loan swing for the pre-Federal Reserve period is highly positively correlated with the loan swing of each particular year in the sample. In other words, banks that had highly variable loans and did not join the Federal Reserve continued to have similarly variable loans. This result shows that the Federal Reserve Bank of New York was "accommodating commerce and business" by discounting and purchasing large quantities of bank loans during the fourth quarter, as noted by Miron (1986). The balance sheet of the Federal Reserve Bank of New York clearly documents this activity. In 1924, for example, the New York Federal Reserve held nearly $200 million of commercial bank loans on its books, which it acquired as collateral for discount loans or purchases in the open market, at the end of the fourth quarter, nearly double the quantity of loans held at the end of the third quarter (FRB NY 1924).

Table 8 also shows that after becoming Federal Reserve members, banks changed the composition of their cash assets, which is not surprising. After 1917, regulations required member banks to hold all of their required reserves at the Federal Reserve. Columns (3) through (6) illustrate this shift. The ratio of cash to assets decreases by 1.5 percent; the ratio of due from banks and the Federal Reserve to assets increases by 1.8 to 2 percent. These increases are substantial in magnitude and statistically significant. The Federal Reserve noted this phenomenon in a statement it released to the press in November 1917 summarizing changes in the Federal Reserve's balance sheet in preceding months (Federal Reserve Board 1917).

After joining the Federal Reserve, banks' ratio of loans to assets also increased. The ratio rose from 4.2 to 4.6 percent, suggesting that membership in the Federal Reserve reduced the liquidity risk of greater lending. The diminished loan swing apparent in Table 8 reflects the behavior of banks serving as correspondents for other institutions, primarily in the central reserve city of New York, but also in other major New York cities.

In Table 9, we consider the same dependent variables as in Table 8, but we divide banks into noncorrespondent banks (in the top panel) and due-to correspondent banks (in the bottom panel). To conserve space, we only report the coefficients relating to Federal Reserve membership. Interestingly, the two types of banks display important differences in their reactions to Federal Reserve membership. Noncorrespondents greatly increased their loans-to-assets and displayed *no change* in their loan seasonality. Lending increased because the Federal Reserve reduced the risks associated with periodic liquidity strains in money markets, allowing commercial banks to accommodate the seasonal demands of their commercial and industrial customers. Due-to correspondent banks that joined the Federal Reserve, in contrast, saw a large and significant decline in their loan swing and no change in their loan-to-asset ratios. The results confirm our previous findings about the role of due-to correspondent member banks as liquidity providers to the network. After the founding of the Federal Reserve, their role as liquidity providers increased, which required them to reduce their liquidity risk, which explains why *their own seasonal lending swing diminished.*

The evidence on changes in the lending behavior of Federal Reserve member banks indicates that noncorrespondent member banks expanded their loans and due-to correspondent member banks reduced their seasonal swing upon joining the Federal Reserve. However, the results in tables 8 and 9 do not show the speed of those changes. We address that question in Table 10 by creating a series of indicator variables that capture behavioral changes according to how many years a member bank had been a Federal Reserve member, compared to banks that had never been a Federal Reserve member. To avoid attempting to identify coefficients on a couple of banks, we drop banks when they were Federal Reserve members for more than five years.

The results in Table 10 show that the change in loan swing (driven by the behavior of due-to correspondent member banks) was not immediate. The effect did not become statistically significant until the third year. This suggests that the effects of Federal Reserve membership in building the due-to correspondent banks' networks were gradual. In contrast, the effect on loans to assets (driven by the behavior of noncorrespondent banks) shows a sudden jump on joining the Federal Reserve. Adjustments of cash and reserves at the Federal Reserve are also quite rapid.

6. Conclusion

We study the slow response of state-chartered banks to the opportunity to join the Federal Reserve System, which began operation in 1914. Initially, very few state banks and trust companies chose to become Federal Reserve members. Even as late as the mid-1920s less than a third of the banks had become Federal Reserve members. This variation in membership choice allows us to examine the factors than influenced membership.

Data for New York suggest that the decision to adopt was based on several factors. The costs of zero-interest reserve requirements of the Federal Reserve appears to have been an important impediment, especially for banks outside of New York City, even after reforms to reserve requirement rules in 1917. But other factors were more important in explaining why some banks within different geographic groupings (for example, banks located outside New York City) chose to become Federal Reserve members but others did not.

Access to the Federal Reserve's discount window — and the greater ability to reduce liquidity risk that such access afforded — seems to have been recognized by state-chartered banks as the primary attraction of joining the Federal Reserve. Banks with relatively high seasonality in their loan demand (and consequently greater liquidity risk) were more likely to join. At the same time, the position of a bank in the correspondent network substantially influenced this benefit of Federal Reserve membership. All other things being equal, small banks located close to a sufficient number of Federal Reserve member banks were less likely to join the Federal Reserve, presumably because they could obtain pass-throughs of Federal Reserve discounting from member banks. Conversely, large banks that occupied important positions in the interbank network were especially willing to become members because access to the Federal Reserve improved their importance as conduits of liquidity to other banks.

We also examine the effects of Federal Reserve membership on lending. These differed for due-to correspondent banks and other banks. For due-to correspondent banks, Federal Reserve membership produced a decrease in the bank's yearly loan variation, consistent with these banks role as liquidity providers. This effect took time to materialize, because it depended on the effect of Federal Reserve membership on the growth of the bank's network. For other banks, joining the Federal Reserve had no effect on the seasonality of lending, but increased the amount of lending. So although nonmember banks could achieve some of the benefits of reduced liquidity risk through pass-throughs from due-to correspondents, indirect access to the discount window was not a perfect substitute for direct access through Federal Reserve membership.

Our results both on the determinants of Federal Reserve membership and its consequences suggest that, consistent with the motives for establishing the Federal Reserve, it was seen by prospective members as an effective means of reducing seasonal liquidity risk and it did, in fact, achieve that end. The data also show that some banks used their access to the Federal Reserve's discount window, and the costs that smaller banks faced in joining the Federal Reserve, as a means of expanding their own role as liquidity providers in the network. Finally, our paper demonstrates that the moral hazard problem of shadow banking was present during the early Federal Reserve era. Many state-chartered banks managed to gain access indirectly to the Federal Reserve's discount window while avoiding the reserve requirements of the Federal Reserve — the regulations that were most important in preventing excess risk taking by banks with access to the discount window.

References

Bernstein, Asaf, Eric Hughson, and Marc Weidenmier. 2010. "Identifying the Effects of a Lender of Last Resort on Financial Markets: Lessons from the Founding of the Fed," *Journal of Financial Economics* 98, 40-53.

Federal Reserve Board. "November 4, 1917," H.4.1 Factors Affecting Bank Reserves and Condition Statement of F.R. Banks (1917-11-04). https://fraser.stlouisfed.org/title/?id=83#!65359, accessed on January 28, 2015.

Bordo, Michael D., Angela Redish, and Hugh Rockoff. 2014. "A Comparison of the Stability and Efficiency of the Canadian and American Banking Systems, 1875-1925," *Financial History Review*, forthcoming.

Calomiris, Charles W., and Mark Carlson. 2014. "Corporate Governance and Risk Management at Unprotected Banks: National Banks in the 1890s," Working paper, September.

Calomiris, Charles W., Mark Carlson, Matthew Jaremski, and Haelim Park. 2014. "Networks, Niches, and Liquidity Risk of National and State-Chartered Banks," Working paper.

Calomiris, Charles W., and Gary Gorton. 1991. "The Origins of Banking Panics: Models, Facts, and Bank Regulation," in R. G. Hubbard, ed., *Financial Markets and Financial Crises*, 109-73. Chicago: University of Chicago Press.

Calomiris, Charles W., and Stephen H. Haber. 2014. *Fragile By Design: The Political Origins of Banking Crises and Scarce Credit*. Princeton: Princeton University Press.

Carlson, Mark, Kris Mitchener, and Gary Richardson. 2014. "Arresting Banking Panics: Federal Reserve Liquidity Provision and the Forgotten Panic of 1929," *Journal of Political Economy* 119, 889-924.

Cannon, James G. 1910. *Clearing Houses*. National Monetary Commission, Senate Document No. 491, 61st Congress, 2nd Session. Washington: Government Printing Office.

Congressional Quarterly. 1923. "Why State Banks Do Not Join the Federal Reserve System, the Effect on the System, and the Issues Involved," *Editorial Research Reports* Vol. I, Washington, D.C.: CQ Press.

Federal Reserve Bank of New York. Annual Report of the Federal Reserve Bank of New York. Various issues 1915 to 1924. https://fraser.stlouisfed.org/title/?id=467, accessed on January 28, 2015.

Federal Reserve Bank of New York. Federal Reserve Bank of New York Circulars. Various issues 1914 to 1924. https://fraser.stlouisfed.org/title/?id=466, accessed on January 28, 2015.

Gorton, Gary. 1985. "Clearinghouses and the Origin of Central Banking in the United States," *Journal of Economic History* 45, 277-83.

Haines, Michael. 2004. "Historical, Demographic, Economic, and Social Data: The United States, 1790-2002 (ICPSR 2896). Inter-University Consortium for Political and Social Research.

Hanes, Christopher, and Paul Rhode. 2013. "Harvests and Financial Crises in Gold-Standard America," *Journal of Economic History* 73, 201-246.

Jaremski, Matthew. 2013. *National Bank Balance Sheets.* Unpublished database collected from the Comptroller of the Currency's *Annual Report.*

Mankiw, N. Gregory, and Jeffrey A. Miron. 1987. "The Adjustment of Expectations to a Change in Regime: A Study of the Founding of the Federal Reserve," *American Economic Review* 77, 358-74.

Miron, Jeffrey A. 1986. "Financial Panics, the Seasonality of the Nominal Interest Rate, and the Founding of the Fed," *American Economic Review* 76, 125-40.

Polks Bankers Encyclopedia, 1901-1910. Chicago: The Bankers Encyclopedia Company.

Rand McNally Bankers' Directory, 1890-1900. Chicago: Rand McNally.

United States Department of Commerce. 1970. Historical Statistics of the United States, Colonial Times to 1970, Part 1. Washington, D.C: Government Printing Office.

United States National Monetary Commission. Publications of the National Monetary Commission. https://fraser.stlouisfed.org/title/?id=1493, November 29, 1909. accessed on January 28, 2015.

United States National Monetary Commission. "Suggested Plan for Monetary Legislation : 61st Congress, 3d Session, Senate Document No. 784" in Suggested Plan for Monetary Legislation : Submitted to the National Monetary Commission (January 16, 1911). https://fraser.stlouisfed.org/title/?id=664#!22042, accessed on January 28, 2015.

United States National Monetary Commission. "Suggested Plan for Monetary Legislation (Revised Edition) : 61st Congress, 3d Session, Senate Document No. 784, Part 2" in Suggested Plan for Monetary Legislation : Submitted to the National Monetary Commission (October 14, 1911). https://fraser.stlouisfed.org/title/?id=664#!22043, accessed on January 28, 2015.

United States National Monetary Commission. January 8,1912. Letter from Secretary of the National Monetary Commission, Transmitting, Pursuant to Law, the Report of the Commission. https://fraser.stlouisfed.org/title/?id=641, accessed on January 28, 2015.

Richardson, Gary, and William Troost. 2009. "Monetary Intervention Mitigated Banking Panics during the Great Depression: Quasi-Experimental Evidence from the Federal Reserve District Border in Mississippi, 1929 to 1933," *Journal of Political Economy* 117, 1031-1073.

Timberlake, Richard. 1984. "The Central Banking Role of the Clearinghouse Associations," *Journal of Money, Credit and Banking* 16, 1-15.

Wall Street Journal. "Country Check Collecting in Federal Reserve Hands." December 28, 1918, p.10.

White, Eugene N. 1983. *The Regulation and Reform of the American Banking System, 1900-1929*. Princeton: Princeton University Press.